I0428972

Prepping: Booby Traps

Prepping And Fortifying Your Home With Booby Traps

By Rick Canton

Copyright 2015 by Rick Canton - All rights reserved.

This document is geared towards providing exact and reliable information in regard to the topic and issue covered. The publication is sold with the idea that the publisher is not required to render accounting, officially permitted, or otherwise, qualified services. If advice is necessary, legal or professional, a practiced individual in the profession should be ordered.

From a Declaration of Principles which was accepted and approved equally by a Committee of the American Bar Association and a Committee of Publishers and Associations.

In no way is it legal to reproduce, duplicate, or transmit any part of this document in either electronic means or in printed format. Recording of this publication is strictly prohibited and any storage of this document is not allowed unless with written permission from the publisher. All rights reserved.

The information provided herein is stated to be truthful and consistent, in that any liability, in terms of inattention or otherwise, by any usage or abuse of any policies, processes, or directions contained within is the solitary and utter responsibility of the recipient reader. Under no circumstances will any legal responsibility or blame be held against the publisher for any reparation, damages, or monetary loss due to the information herein, either directly or indirectly.

Respective authors own all copyrights not held by the publisher.

The information herein is offered for informational purposes solely, and is universal as so. The presentation of the information is without contract or any type of guarantee assurance.

The trademarks that are used are without any consent, and the publication of the trademark is without permission or backing by the trademark owner. All trademarks and brands within this book are for clarifying purposes only and are the owned by the owners themselves, not affiliated with this document.

Table of Contents

Introduction

Any number of situations necessitates the need for extreme survival tactics. As a home owner, you are inevitably aware of how beneficial it can be to maintain a reliable method of security for your home. Whether it is to protect your personal belongings or to protect family members, the integrity of your home should be maintained at all times. With the constant increase in crime throughout the society, finding the appropriate means of home protection can prove to be exponentially advantageous. As a form of protection, booby traps can become a staple security item for a variety of homes across the world. With the help of this e-book, you can prepare your home and loved ones for the worst.

No matter the design, booby traps have two things in common.

First, they look harmless enough that anyone who doesn't look too closely will probably write off the item as something that he should not be too concerned about. Consider small cans lying in a busy sidewalk at various intervals; they don't look misplaced and people who see them won't suspect immediately that there might be a bomb in one of the canisters. Traps are frequently inconspicuous. They're intended to blend with the surroundings.

Secondly, booby traps are intended to do a specific thing to the target, whether it's something that could wound the target (i.e. traps utilized in home security, hunting and combat) or it's merely to elicit a reaction of surprise and enjoyment (like those traps used as practical jokes).

This book was written for anyone with an interest in fortifying his/her home following a natural disaster, the diehard survivalists, and the average homeowner who wants to be prepared against looters and criminals if things turn nasty. As you'll learn, natural disasters can make your home and your loved ones vulnerable to external attack, even after the primary event has occurred.

Using this vital e-book will help you learn how to deter intruders through security measures, common sense techniques, and basic booby traps. In addition to constructing and operating traps, you'll also learn how to construct a safe room should you need to store your survival cache and retreat in the face of danger. Keep reading to see how you could protect your home with some booby traps that would make criminals think twice.

Because instructional images may be difficult to see in the Kindle format, we've included a link to the full list of high-resolution images in the conclusion.

Booby Traps and Prepping Your Property

Booby Traps:

Typically, a booby trap is a triggered device that lures an intruder with the intention of killing, disengaging, or surprising him or her. More often than not, the device is triggered by the victim himself or herself unknowingly. These devices date from ancient times and history shows us that booby traps have been used by the great Pharaohs of Egypt and their aides who trusted in their efficiency - they even used them to secure their tombs. Apparently, these devices show how ingenious the human mind really is. In this e-book, we describe booby traps and techniques that are intended to protect you and your home from a direct threat to your safety. In an extreme survival situation, a threat is anyone attempting to enter your property without permission and with criminal intent. This includes thieves, looters, or gangs in the wake of natural or social upheaval. When the worst comes, you can be prepared. Booby traps can also be used to trap wild animals and other creatures you don't want around your house.

There's no telling when a severe upheaval or disaster will occur. Natural, social, and economic disasters can lead to a scenario where your home, family, food and weapons can come under threat; that's where our traps come in. But first, you'll need to learn how to be watchful for signs of impending disaster. To keep an eye out for a looming disaster, monitor weather forecasts for news about severe weather conditions. Natural disasters include droughts, forest fires, flooding, tsunamis, avalanches, hurricanes, tornados, earthquakes, volcanoes, and mud flows. Arguably, social and economic disasters are harder to predict, though many news sources can be monitored if rioting or other extreme behavior begins to spread.

When social disaster strikes, the booby trap is an excellent method for deterring these threats because it avoids direct violence. Booby traps are effective in both a home invasion situation and a survival one. During a home invasion usually the attacker has the element of surprise; you realize you're under attack when the attacker (s) is (are) already in the house. If you install a couple of intricate and cleverly hidden devices in your yard, you may ruin their plan and be alerted in time of their intentions. Booby traps are really useful to have around your house as they serve these main purposes:

- To scare and intimidate an intruder that is faint of heart. This way you'll get rid of attackers that are not prepared to engage in close body combat without even having to confront them;
- To delay the assailant and raise the alarm that someone is trying to barge in;
- To hurt and/or trap the intruder in a place where it's safe to confront him (or her);
- To protect your assets from curious snoopers (of course, this means the device is going to be smaller and meant to scare).

Though the name may sound a bit comical, as you can see, but this device really means serious business – booby traps are inherently dangerous. With this type of contraption, you can actually kill someone so make sure you know what you want to do with it before thinking about installing one. Before you consider arming your home against intruders, there are several important factors to ponder. Consider how secure your home is and whether or not lethal traps are likely to provoke future, more intent intruders. The last thing you want is to have your security system create more problems. Also consider whether or not they are necessary at all. We recommend that unless you are in immediate danger, it's best to employ non-lethal methods.

Prepping Your Property:

Preparing or prepping your property for booby traps is the first step toward a disaster-ready home. When prepping your property, first consider when your home will be most vulnerable. Often, this is at night and when you're away. Even if you're a night owl who seldom leaves their house, there are still ways those who wish to harm you or exploit your property can carry out their plans. Intruders can easily determine when you're away by monitoring refuse collection, lighting, and other habitual activities. Also consider the weakest points of your property. Ask yourself this – where are intruders most likely to enter your home? Where is the lowest number of security measures? Often, the garage is the weakest point of a property because it's easy to forget about locking, and it's often located at the edge of a property so someone trying to break in is likely to attract less attention. Garages often come equipped with a number of windows as well, and windows are also a weak spot because they can be broken easily.

Before implementing lethal traps, consider non-lethal forms of defense, including guard dogs, CCTV, motion sensors and lights. If you have more time, consider growing thorn bushes or thick foliage around your property. A more unorthodox approach to an alarm system that might sound strange is the use of geese, which make a lot of noise when disturbed and can act as an effective warning system. You can transform your windows from a weak spot to a security measure; consider reinforcing your windows with bulletproof or tempered glass and strengthening your doors with door bars and additional locks (You'll find more about this in chapter 8).

Trip Wires

Trip Wire Info:

Many people worry about the expensive home burglar alarm system they have to buy for their home security in order to feel or stay safe and the need to spend even more money just for the security company to install the alarm. Even more money have to be spent if you add in the monthly cost of monitoring by home security providers. But aside from these sophisticated CCTV cameras and expensive alarm systems, trip wires are one of the best ways you can easily be alerted when someone is trying to enter your property without your knowledge or consent. The trip wire is an alert-based trap that works by the intruder activating an alarm by walking across the wire. The trip wire is actually used to set up the actual trap or the alarm. Like most home safety devices, trip wires are prompted by sensors. The principle behind this device is easy and very simple to put into practice: you set up the trap (or the alarm) and install a wire that when interrupted or disturbed sets up the end device. Once the alarm has been triggered, this gives you time to act. You have a number of options when an alarm sounds via trip wire, but you have to think quickly! Often the safest option is retreat to your safe room or another secure location (see chapter 8). You will also have time to contact the police or other help. The very last resort if an intruder is on the way and there is no help in sight is to prepare yourself to challenge the intruder though this should *always* be the last resort.

There are numerous different types of trip wires, including remote trip wire alarms, foghorn trip wires and explosive trip wires. Explosive trip wires are not mines or otherwise lethal types of traps; rather, they use simple explosives to create a loud noise and a flash that is not directly harmful to the intruder.

Setting up a trip wire requires only simple common sense and safety procedures. The best time to set a trip wire is in daylight, making sure it's discreet as possible. Take care to set the trap along a route that an intruder is likely to take if attempting to enter your property. Also, mark where the trip wire has been set and tell other people in your group to be sure you or other innocent people don't activate the wire by accident.

How to Build:

For trip wires to work effectively they must be discreet, both before activation and after. Although it's important for your loved ones to be able to detect your trip wires, an intruder must not be able to detect the trap easily. For this e-book, we describe how to construct a remote trip wire, which is often the most effective and can be made easily and cheaply.

First, select a small wireless transmitter to activate the alarm. Almost all radios contain transmitters that can work over long distances; these would be viable options for trip wires located some distance from your house. You can also use the transmitter in a wireless doorbell, which is ideal for short-range alarm trip wires. Aside from their short-range capabilities and use near the homestead, wireless doorbell transmitters are also a good choice because it is discreet, battery-powered, easy to program, and several transmitters can activate a single receiver. Walkie Talkies and wireless garage door openers can also provide the necessary electronics for effective trip wires.

Take two pieces of wires at least three inches long and remove the insulation from both ends of each piece. Remove the housing on the transmitter and solder one end of each wire to two of the button terminals. If your button has four terminals, solder the wires to the terminals that are not connected to the button. You can use a multimeter to check which terminals are connected and which aren't.

Once you have sorted the terminals, the next job is to make a switch that can be activated when the tripwire is pulled. The switch is surprisingly inexpensive; you can make a spring-loaded switch out of a standard wooden clothes peg. To complete the switch, you will also need two machine screws and two nuts (as shown).

First, disassemble the clothes peg and drill holes in each end of the wood that usually grips the clothes. The drill hole should be the same diameter as the screws. Insert the screws through the holes with the head of the screw on the inside of the peg. Loosely screw a nut onto the outside end of each screw to hold it in place. Now, drill a hole in the other end of the peg and reassemble.

When you finish creating the switch, attach the wires from the transmitter to the clothes peg switch by wrapping the free end of the wires around the screws underneath the nuts. Tighten the nuts to secure the wire in place. Whenever the clothes peg is closed, the transmitter will be activated.

Once the trip wire is assembled, you need to decide on a location for your trip wire. The best location is a narrow pathway or trail where traffic is restricted. Remember, think like an intruder; the pathway should be one that you suspect an intruder will take. Choose a point on the pathway that is surrounded by vegetation on each side since the trip wire needs to be mounted approximately one foot from the ground.

Cut a length of fishing wire, or other translucent plastic wire, and tie one end to the additional hole you drilled through the clothes peg. To secure the switch, tie the other end to a structure close to the pathway such as a tree or shrub. Cut a second length of trip wire and run it across the pathway. Tie one end to a structure on the other side of the pathway. Then attach a small square of flat plastic measuring 1 inch by 1 inch to the other end of the trip wire. Take this end to the clothes peg and slide the plastic square between the two screw end contacts. This way, when someone walks into the trip wire across the path, the plastic square is pulled away and the screws make contact, which activates the transmitter, which in turn activates the tone on the doorbell receiver. To ensure the invader trips the alarm and does not see it before it's too late, be sure to hide the doorbell transmitter well in the undergrowth.

Keep in mind that the doorbell transmitter and receiver will have a limited range. Test the range before setting the trip wire. Depending on your preference, the receiver tone can be modified, or an LED can be installed if you prefer a silent alarm.

External Deterrents

Deterrent Info:

The first thing that comes to most people's mind when talking about home security is the alarm systems. However, there is much more to securing your home than calling in your local alarm installer. Unless you probably live in a bank vault, there's hardly a way you can prevent a determined crook from breaking into your home but most criminals aren't that determined, they're just looking for an easy score.

Deterrents are classified as anything that gives intruders pause before nearing your home. Simple deterrents in the grounds of your property can also be effective in addition to trip wires, especially if you feel particularly under threat. Barbed wire, razor wire, chicken wire, perimeter fences or electrified fencing makes it difficult for intruders to gain access to your home and serve as a visual deterrent as well. The first key discriminator for burglars when it comes to choosing which house in the street to rob is the presence of visual deterrents. Home security visual deterrents include external intelligent lighting, external home security alarm system monitoring warning signs, lockable gates, garages and/or sheds, visible and audible alarms, CCTV cameras, home security screens, active neighbors and our faithful hounds.

External alarm boxes are a good deterrent. Just having an alarm system installed by a recognized intruder alarm installer should deter most villains, whether they are opportunists or professionals. After all, burglars don't know whether or not your system is monitored by a central station who will alert the Police in the instance of an alarm - it's easier for them to go next door or somewhere that doesn't have an alarm system.

Knowing that the alarm will alert the homeowner or authorities and severely limit his time, may be too high a risk for him. Even if you don't install an alarm system, signs alone can be effective. In many cases, yard signs and window stickers indicating a monitored security system is active are enough to turn a crook away. A comprehensive home security strategy starts with external deterrents. In order to provide a base level of home security, external security deterrents are a necessity. Often, simply placing a security alarm warning sign in a prominent place at the front of your premises is a great idea, but with external deterrents, whether your home is fitted with an alarm or not, external deterrents will most likely get your house struck off the burglars list. External deterrents are a powerful tool in your home security arsenal and do not have to include expensive technologies.

External (and visual) deterrents are your first level of security protection and the first features of your residence to be examined by the burglar. Motion activated lighting around your house is a good deterrent. Lights in the driveway and near doors and windows can startle a criminal. Bad guys prefer darkness. Light increases the chance they will be seen. While many burglaries are spontaneous, opportunistic crimes can be prevented by external deterrents. Many burglaries are also well planned team events in which the perpetrators have conducted significant field research into your neighborhood and most importantly your property. The professional burglar does his homework and the first step in his decision making process is the elimination of unnecessary risk. Make your house look like someone is home even when you are away. Leave interior lights on in rooms that are normally lit when you are home. To be more convincing, put lights on a timer. This will likely deter him from intruding into your property.

How to Build a Perimeter Fence:

Before you build a perimeter fence, you need to find out whether there is any legal regulation in your area for fence building. Furthermore, it is also important to figure out the measurements of each of the fences dimensions and always take into consideration any obstruction in the area that may hinder the construction of the fence. When you have already figured out the length and style of the fence you want to build, you can start purchasing materials. Your choice of materials is of course, dependent on the fences primary purpose – deterring crooks from getting in – and your budget in relation to what you want to construct. There are different types of fences available in the market, from chain fences to privacy fences that come in different prices and styles. You could check out local fence stores or stores supplying home-improvement items. The best materials include block, wood, vinyl and metal. These kinds of fence materials are more suitable to keep unwanted trespassers out.

After you have selected your fence, you need to dig holes with clamshell diggers at the right places in your garden to put up the posts (or concrete blocks). Putting some gravel under the areas where you would be setting the posts would be a great idea, to prevent the posts from decaying, hence easy removal. Then, trim the posts to level them after putting them up.

Then put barbed wire around the fence. Barbed wire or line fences do not re□uire much support as posts or wooden fences. You will need to varnish, paint and maintain the wooden fences every year, and prevent the rusting of the barbed wires. In this respect, privacy fences and invisible fences are low maintenance, as you do not have to constantly maintain or paint them. Another important factor to take into account is the height of the fence. Building a fence secured by barb wires is useless if it can easily be scaled by a common dog.

The other inexpensive fencing options are the waffle and the cleft chestnut, which look more like some kind of a basket and give a rustic look to your house. However, these fencing types are very strong and remain so for a longer period of time. Alternatively you could purchase a Do-It-Yourself (DIY) kit from a local hobby store. These are inexpensive and come with special instructions and a warranty.

Most importantly, you should always make sure that you comply with the local codes and laws to avoid complications. It is important to also check any neighborhood zoning ordinance and obtain necessary permits before starting on establishing the design. Overall, many factors should be considered first before building and designing a fence. Doing so, you can never go wrong with the aforementioned reminders.

Similarly, you can put together a surveillance deterrent for your home security. As mentioned earlier, this will provide adequate and cost effective security solutions.

Setting up a Surveillance/Visual Deterrent:

Depending on your budget you can follow all of the steps – each of the following sections will be a series of steps that can build upon each other – or you can stop whenever you think the protection will be sufficient enough and will stay within your means.

Step 1 - Surveillance Signs

This is the first and foremost deterrent to burglars and intruders in the surveillance world. This one piece of CCTV e□uipment can help deter and stop a vast majority of would-be interlopers. When using surveillance signs you provide a very visual warning to people that there's surveillance on the premises and it would be in their best interest to leave it alone. Even if you don't have a surveillance system, most criminals aren't going to know this, and aren't likely to try and ascertain as to whether it's true.

When using surveillance signs there are several key areas you will want to post them. Firstly, you will want to make sure to have one located at each point of entry into your home or business. This way the criminal is sure to see them no matter where they try to break in at. Secondly if you have any form of property, then it is a good idea to place signs on the perimeter of your land. By doing this you may deter a criminal before they even set foot on your property. Lastly, if you have a main floor window that is on a side of the building without any form of conventional entryway, it is a good idea to place a sign in this window as well; just in case the intruder tries to break in through the window.

As far as price goes when purchasing surveillance signs, it can be the most inexpensive aspect of surveillance deterrents. Generally surveillance signs will come in packs of 2 and cost cheaply. Depending on how many areas you need to cover, you can generally cover them all for under a 100 dollars.

Step 2 - Dummy Cameras

After procuring your surveillance signs, you're ready to take your visual deterrents to the next level and install a few dummy cameras. Dummy cameras are simply the shells of actual security cameras made to be used as a visual deterrent to intruders. By having a few of these placed around your home or business you are providing a second piece of visual evidence that will make a trespasser think twice about what they're doing.

Dummy cameras are most affective when placed near your main entry points so as to build upon the surveillance sign deterrents. This way not only will the criminal see your surveillance sign, but they will also see the dummy camera backing up what your sign is proclaiming. So if the criminal wasn't convinced beforehand, they most likely will be at this point.

When it comes to pricing, dummy cameras also come cheaply usually between 30 and 50 dollars, so if you get one for both the front and back of your building this will cost just under 100 dollars. Additionally, sites such as CU1.com or maybe even your local surveillance installers offer dead security cameras for very cheap price (between 10 and 20 dollars). These may no longer function as a normal security cameras, but they can easily serve as a dummy camera.

Step 3 - Add a Single Camera System

After you've set yourself up with these visual deterrents you may now want the ability to record and monitor at least one area, just in case the visual deterrents aren't enough. In this circumstance, I would recommend a single channel system with the ability to upgrade in the future. This way you can cover your most sensitive area and then expand your monitoring capabilities should the need arise.

This single camera system should be used to monitor your main entryway or any problem area you may have had in the past. As far as cost is concerned, it can vary, but a good recommendation is the DigiairWatch by Securityman. That system is a single channel system that has the capability of adding up to 3 more cameras for a 4 camera system.

Step 4 - When The Budget Expands

The first 3 steps are good ways to provide protection on your property against most criminal elements, and to do so within a budget. In the future however if you still feel the need for more protection, I would suggest either upgrading your single-channel system into a 4-channel system, or I would suggest contacting a professional surveillance installer to help you with designing a system that will fully monitor and protect your facilities. This will be a bit more costly, but it may be what you need in heavier crime invested areas.

A decent surveillance system for a small business or home will generally cost hundreds of dollars but depending on how large of a system you want, it can drastically increase from there. In the end, if you are very budget conscience and you just want to help prevent something before it happens, then for around 200 dollars you can get a good number of surveillance signs, dummy cameras and for a little extra a single channel surveillance kit.

Pit Traps

Pit Traps Info:

There are also more invasive techniques for protecting your home starting with the grounds, which includes traps with the intention of doing serious harm. More serious traps that are particularly vicious include the swinging log trap with or without spikes, the spring spear trap, rock spring with spikes, the spike pit, and numerous others. Not only do these traps hurt and impale the intruder's foot, the trap gets his/her ankle as well as lowering his/her leg too.

As we mentioned before in this book, these traps should only be used in extreme situations and should be set with care. Note that, it is illegal to construct these traps on your property during peace time. Additionally, if they are required and need to be built, use extreme caution; they are lethal to human life and should not be constructed alone. These traps are designed for use in extreme conditions such as a natural disaster or widespread social upheaval. They should be employed as a means of defense against external threats to your survival.

These pit traps are not ideal for all locations; most of these traps are ideal for property owners with surrounding trees, woodland, or undergrowth. These kinds of terrain are perfect for hiding traps to disengage threats. Pitfall spear traps can be dug at various locations around your property along points you suspect intruders will take. For pit traps and spear traps, the best place to site them is on footpaths, under steps, in rubble or foliage, and at the base of walls and fences. While pit and spear traps are effective at deterring single-person threats, log traps and spring spear traps can deter groups or gangs.

How to Build:

For any of the traps mentioned, it's a good idea to channel intruders along a single path through the woods using either fences or shrubs. Site your traps along the path, preferably in a clearing.

We'll start simple. The pit is probably the easiest trap to build. Dig a pit measuring 3 foot squared and 3 foot deep. Fill the pit with secured, sharpened sticks and cover with small twigs and branches that will break under foot.

An invisible hook trap can tangle potential intruders as well. If you have foliage close to your home, hang heavy-gauge monofilament fishing wire from branches at six-inch intervals. Attach fishing hooks to the ends of the line and hang the hooks at roughly waist height. When they encounter the trap, intruders will quickly become entangled and will be unlikely to come closer to your home.

Trapping Plants

Trapping Plants Info:

There are many different types of plants, trees, shrubs and bushes you can arrange around your home that can offer some of the best lines of defense against intruders, burglars and bad guys. With so many high tech cameras and security systems, services and providers to choose from when setting up a home security system for you and your family on the indoors, it's important to remember that outdoor plants, if placed and maintained appropriately, can provide an another cost effective way to deter intruders. Usually a one time cost, certain plants that include thorns and spikes are a great way to set up an outside perimeter of barbed wire vegetation that will guarantee a second thought of entry onto your property. There's nothing like hurting the ones who dare to hide within your perimeter, scoping out your private space and waiting to make a move. We'll go over the different types of plants that are extremely beneficial and effective when setting up an outdoor home security perimeter.

Setting up Trapping Plant/Types of Plants

Thorny plants like cactus' or blackberry hedges are perfect for your house defense. Intruders who have the bad luck of stumbling into one of these plants will not be very happy, and chances are they will forget why they were there in the first place as they whimper away in pain. These plants can grow over and through fences, have spiny branches and grow about 5-6 feet tall. Although, some intruders will not be bothered by them, however, most burglars in their right mind would give your house a second thought.

The Pyracantha (aka the fire thorn bush) is another great deterrent. Its sharp barbed leaves act just as barbed wire would around a prison yard. Rose bushes and Voodoo rose bushes under windows also add a touch of style to your home security needs when it comes to looks. Not only are they beautiful, the thorny stems and leaves are not something anyone wants to be attacked by. The wounds that these plants gives, sting and burn once the skin is broken which causes the skin to become itchy and a major distraction for the intruder. Plus, once the skin is broken and itchy, the problem increases as the itchiness can spread easily.

The Oregon grape holly is another friend to us but enemy to an intruder. It has spiked leaves that look like tiny biting teeth and it grows upward, running along the edges of your home or along fencing on your outside perimeters. Similarly, the Washington hawthorn has amazing 3" spiked thorns that could literally stop an intruder in its tracks, regardless of their pain tolerance. The Washington hawthorn can grow up to and over 30 feet over periods of time, plus it has a very nice curb appeal.

So what do you take from this? Are you going to go out and buy the most harmful plants? Well, hold on. It's important you don't get carried away when deciding how many and which types of plants you're going to fill your yard(s) with. You truly don't want the thick shrubbery that will add too much privacy to your home or give an intruder an opportunity to hide while waiting to make a move. It's more important that all walkways, door entries and windows are 100% visible for you and to your neighbors. Spotting an unwelcome guest before it's too late could be crucial in certain situations, and if you're giving them room to hide just on the inside of the perimeter, well, you really haven't deterred anyone.

Also, when you get ready to start planting trees that are large, or will grow to be large, make sure there is enough room or a gap between the branches and the roof of homes, second story windows and balconies as well as neighbors roofs, windows and balconies can be easily reached if the branches are thick and too close to the dwellings. Trimming back branches and shrubbery can eliminate easy access ways to your home, as well as your neighbors homes. Another thing to keep in mind is if you have basement windows, try not to have too much vegetation growing along these sides of your house. Instead, line the perimeter of your yard and walkways with low, thin plants.

Internal Perimeter Deterrents

Deterrent Info:

If for some reason, the intruders have ways to avoid the exterior traps, there are also methods for protecting your home should intruders make it past your external security measures. Many of these can be incorporated into the exterior of your property and serve as a last line of defense before intruders gaining access to your home.

How to Build:

Tire spikes or nails can be enough to deter intruders from entering your home. Drive nails into a section of plywood and site boards on the ground at all of the ground floor entrances. To ensure both your windows and ground floor doors are effectively secure, Glass or nails can be set in cement or glued on the tops of walls and on window ledges to deter those seeking entry through windows.

To incorporate glass into your deterrents, break old glass bottles, jars, or other glass items into inch long shards using a hammer. Then, spread clear silicone or glue over the intended area and place pieces of glass with the sharp edges facing up. If you are seeking a more organic approach to perimeter security, another useful deterrent is, oddly enough, plants. Place cacti and other thorny or impenetrable plants in large pots in front of windows and other weak spots.

It is possible to electrify windows sills and door knobs, though many burglars and criminals wear gloves so the electric current would have little effect. Beware that electrifying entranceways in your home is illegal and should only be used in extreme situations. It's a better idea to buy electrified fencing from a local farm supplier.

If you are intent on electrifying vulnerable points, the capacitor from a disposable camera can be used.

To create an electrified deterrent, dismantle the camera and discharge the capacitor. This is the large black battery-like cylinder inside the camera flash housing. Safety is paramount; Touch both prongs of the capacitor with the metal end of an insulated screwdriver to discharge. This is important since the capacitor can retain electric charge and could lead to electrocution. Once the capacitor has been discharged, you can handle the components freely.

The next step is to create a basic circuit either using proto-board or as a standalone circuit. You have most of the components you need aside from the proto-board; the basic circuit consists of a capacitor, transformer, transistor, resistor, and diode, all of which can be taken from the camera circuit.

To assemble the electrification unit, you will need a soldering iron and some solder to attach the transistor base to pin 4 of the transformer and then solder the transistor's collector to pin 1 of the transformer.

Next, solder one of the resistor's lead to pin 2 of the transformer and solder the other resistor lead to pin 3 of the transformer. Solder the cathode lead of the diode to pin 5 of the transformer.

Next, solder one of the capacitor's leads to the anode of the diode and solder the other lead of the capacitor to pin 2 of the transformer. Solder the 0v of the battery to the transistor's emitter and solder the positive voltage of the battery to pin 2 of the transformer.

Now you can solder the high voltage output wire to the cathode of the diode and the capacitor. This may seem complicated but there are numerous online guides if you run into trouble.

The final step is to install a switch and attach two 5 inch strips of magnet wire to the positive and negative outputs of the transformer. Now you can attach the circuit to a door knob, or window handle. Attach two

1 inch by 1/8 inch strips of aluminum tape to the handle or knob, one on either side. Attach each end of the magnet wire to the aluminum strips.

Once assembly is complete, you can mount the circuit board close to the door knob using tape. As with any security measure or deterrent on your property, make sure to disguise the circuit board so it resembles something innocuous.

Your electrified components shouldn't take much power to operate. You can use a single 1.5v AA battery to power the circuit. Also note that camera circuits won't deliver a lethal charge, but they can provide a sharp shock to deter intruders.

Internal Deterrents

Deterrent Info:

As you'll learn in the next chapter, a safe room is an excellent idea if you are facing extreme conditions and fear intruders in your home. Once you aware that an intruder has broken in, the best thing to do is to retreat to a safe room or secure place. You should also notify help as soon possible.

However, a safe room is not the only option, and placing traps inside the home may be necessary to ensure the safety of your family, yourself and your property. It might also be a good idea to have booby traps in place inside your home, though beware that traps set out to harm people are illegal, whether inside or outside the home. The traps should only be used as a last resort in an extreme survival situation.

Whether you think it's possible or not, there is a chance an intruder can evade your exterior and interior perimeter defenses. In the unlikely scenario that an intruder compromises the security measures you already have in place, and gains access to the inside of your property, you'll need procedures in place to defend yourself, your family, and your supplies.

Internal deterrents are those things designed to keep an intruder out of your home after evading the exterior perimeters. An interior trap of some sort is a critical part of an effective home security system. You don't want plants and trees to provide cover for the crook, but thorny bushes and shrubs planted under windows can make intrusion attempts quite difficult and painful. The more difficult you make it for the crook to break in increases his chances of being caught. For example, aside from the remote trip wire, you should also consider a silent trip wire alarm inside your house, so you know if and when you've been compromised.

A motion detector is commonly used in the living area as a means of catching an intruder that happened to get by the perimeter protection. The most popular detection devices for your interior include the PIR (Passive Infra-Red) detectors, magnetic reed contacts, breaking glass detectors, infra-red beams, pressure pads, case wiring, vibration detectors and dual technology sensors (sensors that combine Passive Infra-Red with Microwave or Ultrasonic detection). Pet motions are also available in different sizes that will detect intruders but filter out the animals. These pet motions are not recommended for homeowners with cats however. This is because a cat can jump so quickly, as they are known to do, and fool the motion into thinking it is a person standing up. A good alternative in this case is to use an interior door contact on a closet or bedroom door that is kept shut. When the burglar opens that door, the alarm goes off. However, this contact is off when the alarm is armed in the stay mode so that you can go about your business without fear of setting the alarm off.

With that in mind, there are also numerous kinds of basic booby traps that can be used in the home. These include spikes, deadfall traps, trapdoors, fake flooring or steps, and more elaborate traps.

How to Build:

Start by building defenses at the weakest points of your house. Since windows are vulnerable points on any house, setting traps just underneath the window may be effective in deterring intruders. You can prevent intrusion via window much in the same way you arm the other ground floor entrances of your home. Set some spikes, glass, or other sharp materials on the ground and lay cardboard over the top of the spikes. This will deter an intruder from stepping in through a window.

In addition to hidden spikes on the bottom of door frames, a basic trip-release deadfall trap or tiger trap can be constructed above door frames to deter intruders from moving from one room to another (following the same principles as shown in the image).

Essentially, this deadfall traps work by releasing a heavy weight onto the victim when a trip wire is crossed. All you'll need to construct this is some fishing wire and a large weight (any piece of furniture or bulky pot or pan will do). As with all trap setups, exercise caution, especially with potentially incapacitating security measures. Setting the trigger mechanism can be difficult and you are unlikely to get it right first time. Since this is a trap that calls for heavy weights, it may require two or more people to suspend the weight above the door frame or entranceway. As with trip wires, the deadfall trap uses a trip release line that runs just above the ground at the doorway.

Alternatively, a simple snare trap or a trip wire can be used to entangle an intruder. In fact, you can set multiple snares or wires to slow intruders down. For the snare, use wire, paracord, or string to make a simple noose. To create the most effective snare trap, set the noose at ankle height and secure the snare to a fixed structure like a banister or post.

To buy you time if intruders do break into your home, stock physical deterrents like pepper spray and mace. Pepper spray can be made easily and inexpensively. After spraying an intruder, you can retreat to your safe room and contact help. As a new form of protection, pepper spray alarms have become a staple security item for a variety of homes across the world. An added benefit of a pepper spray booby trap is that it provides far more security than a generic alarm system. With the average alarm installation, an alarm will sound and it will alert the police. Although this can prove to be a reasonable method for a variety of families, the time in between the police response and the alarm signal provides more than an ample amount of time for the criminal to gain entry to your home. With the implementation of a pepper spray alarm, the criminal will be automatically disabled rather than forcing you to wait for the law officials to travel to your house.

And, if that wasn't enough, the pepper spray alarms are extremely useful in guarding the contents of mobile homes, RVs, storage buildings, summer homes etc. where law enforcement is not close by and no power supply is available. The unit does not re□uire power or a telephone line. Although an autodialer is recommended to alert you to unusual activity in your property, the pepper spray alarm will force the intruders out before they get anything. These two items work together quite well if you can change the batteries on the autodialer when needed.

Pepper spray alarms have become an exponentially popular choice of security for a variety of families due to the fact that it provides an extra type of protection to a home or even an office building. With the implementation of these systems you can rest assured that your personal belongings and dear family members will be kept safe throughout the day and throughout the night. Rather than having to wait for the police to arrive at your front door, you will be able to immediately stop the burglary so that every family member is kept safe and that no items are stolen within that time frame.

Also, stash some heavy blunt weapons about your house. These blunt instruments might include baseball or cricket bats.

As explained earlier, burglars and indeed any intruders, are overwhelmingly deterred by a burglar alarm more than any other form of home security. A local alarm siren can be ear-splittingly nerve racking to a criminal who is already nervous. A monitored alarm system will also alert a central monitoring station. An operator will receive the call and notify the homeowner to verify the alarm. If the homeowner can't be reached or the password can't be verified they will immediately contact emergency services and send help.

Internal deterrents may also include things that make noise to startle, scare, or irritate the nerves of a crook. First on this list would be a vicious-sounding dog. It can be real or recorded. Either way, it's quite startling and pretty scary.

Building a Safe Room

Safe Room Info:

As we've mentioned before, building a safe room is one of the safest options for you in case of home invasion, disastrous weather or natural conditions. Determining whether or not you need a safe room depends on your perceived risk; where does the risk come from? For example, the risk could come from extreme weather such as tornadoes, hurricanes, earthquakes, and tsunamis. Hurricanes are intermittent. We saw a rash of them hit the US in 2004 and 2005. We saw and many experienced, the ravages of these events. Homes, today, are built to withstand some very high winds - however they are designed to meet the medium sized storm events. Your home might be built "to code" but that does not mean it can withstand the intense winds from the events of a tornado or major hurricane, for example. Frankly, a Category 4 or 5 storm can still destroy a home; even if built to today's standards.

Evacuation is still the best way to avoid the full impact of these mega storms. However if one is unable to get out there is a way to provide some larger degree of safety - and that is by creating a safe room. These are also called storm shelters.

What is a safe room? A safe room is usually an ultra secure location within the home or a building designated to provide shelter for a family during burglary, terrorist attacks and/or other unspecific threats. A safe room usually has special walls, ceilings, fastening systems and doors and are extremely strong (in engineering terms). They can offer the vital purpose of providing safety for you and your loved ones during those scary events.

After going through a natural disaster, a safe room can relieve some of the anxiety that builds up during the threat of an oncoming tornado or hurricane. The purpose of the safe room is to provide a room where you can seek refuge that provides protection for you and your loved ones. Having a safe room in your home or business provides excellent protection against injury or death, either as a direct result of extreme weather conditions or because of intruders or perceived violence. This room can be built in one of several places in your home:

- A Master closet in a bedroom.
- Any bathroom in your home.
- The utility room.
- The basement of your home.
- Any interior room on the first floor.
- On any concrete slab-on-grade foundation or
- Your garage.

You should also consider how feasible it is to construct a safe room. Safe room design varies enormously, depending on the risks involved, space and other factors but generally, safe rooms are windowless and are designed and constructed to withstand and resist the effects of huge pressures – usually 250 miles per hour winds and the impact from windborne debris generated by extremely severe weather. Apparently, this protects the residents of the house from the forceful winds and heavy wind-blown debris.

At the elaborate end of the scale, safe rooms are built into the initial blueprints of houses and might include a wall of surveillance monitors for viewing the perimeters of the building, a kitchenette for cooking, comfortable furnishings, integrated air ventilation, and a sophisticated communications system. Similarly, safe rooms are usually stocked with emergency and survival items. These items should include a flashlight, batteries, water, packaged foods, a first-aid kit, blankets, and a portable toilet. Make no mistake that safe rooms are a long-term investment. Safe rooms like the aforementioned can cost tens of thousands of dollars. However, a well-functioning and secure room for retreat in times of danger can be built on a budget.

For some people, a safe room is seen as an unnecessary retreat from confrontation, especially since many Americans feel capable in their ability to defend their homes through more direct means. However, there are some disasters and intruders that are best handled by retreat. Following the catastrophic disaster of the extent seen in the wake of Hurricane Katrina in New Orleans of 2005, raiding houses and armed conflict could easily escalate beyond your control. What's more, if you have vulnerable family members in your household, such as children or elderly relatives, it's a good idea to a have a secure room in which you can shelter and survive until help arrives. Another reason for constructing a safe room is to stash your valuables there; locked away from intruders.

Safe rooms are not panic rooms. Rather than the name "panic room" suggesting a place of desperation, a "safe room" describes a familiar and secure location that avoids the direct threat posed by an unwelcome visitor. A safe room is intended as a place to stay for a brief period, until it is safe enough to venture out.

Remember, use logic and common sense; do not leave your safe room until you are sure it's safe to do so.

Burglars and home invaders are not movie characters. They are a real threat. We all hope that housebreak will never take place. But no matter how, whether you live in a bad neighborhood or not, it might happen. In such a case, cooperating with the burglars is the last thing you should think about or do.

You should always make sure that all members of your family know how and when to use your safe room. Instruct your children about the importance and the purpose of the room. This room should never be their playground.

Make sure that the emergency cell phone is regularly charged and the flashlights have new batteries. Keep the keys to open the safety room inside. While inside, under siege, call the police and do not exit till they arrive. Again: do not cooperate with the burglars. Don't take their word even if they promise you that once you come out you will be safe. Wait inside for the police.

Safe Room Location:

Safe rooms can be in-residence or in the basement. In-residence ones are favored over cellars and community shelters as they are within seconds of reach and can also be put to other daily uses.

If you're building a house from scratch and want to include a safe room in your design, you have many more options than those constructing a safe room in a house that's already built. However, most readers won't be in the process of building a house and need an affordable alternative to building from scratch.

There are more options than you might think in making an existing room into a safe room for you and your family. A walk-in closet, pantry, en suite bedroom, basement/cellar, storeroom, or garage can all be transformed into an effective safe room, though any space can be used providing it meets the following basic criteria. The basic criteria for safe room creation are the room shouldn't have any windows to the outside and the walls should be thick or reinforced. Also, it should be well ventilated and there should be a water supply and basic bathroom facilities. Finally, there should be enough space for the number of people you expect to shelter there and the room should be easily accessible from several locations in your house.

If you're on a tight budget, consider choosing a smaller room to save money on reinforcing the walls. The best safe room is located in a covert place that is not obvious to intruders. Remember that your safe room can revert to its primary function when not being used as a safe room; this conversion to original function makes the safe room seem even more innocuous.

Safe Room Construction:

The door is your first line of defense against intruders should they attempt to enter. For this reason, the door should be reinforced with a tough material like steel. Exterior doors are much stronger than interior doors, which can be broken down without too much effort. When it comes to securing the entrance to your safe room, exterior steel slab doors are best.

Remember; you want the safe room to be unnoticed as such. Paint your door to match other internal doors so it doesn't stand out. If you have a sturdy door you'll also need a sturdy frame. Replace your standard interior frames with reinforced steel frames; much like interior doors, the interior frames are not nearly as strong as their exterior counterparts. Hang your door so it opens inward. As well as the standard doorknob lock, a heavy duty reinforced deadbolt system might also be a good idea. For extra security you can install a jimmy-proof security lock and an unobtrusive door bar.

More often than not, solid reinforced concrete is the building material of choice for safe rooms that have the ability to withstand the fury of a Rita or a Katrina, talk-less of a crook. Storm damage can often result in leaks and mildew. Solid reinforced concrete offers protections against these. It also offers protection against burrowing animals and pests such as termites. With energy costs ever inching northward, it makes sense to build safe rooms of solid reinforced concrete that maximizes energy efficiency by virtue of its ability to reflect light and having thermal mass. Also solid reinforced concrete are fire and heat resistant and provide greater levels of safety as it does not burn or bend.

If your only option for a safe room is a room with windows, don't worry, they can be reinforced to prevent breakage. To make a security measure out of a weak window, begin by removing and filling in the window, or replacing it with bulletproof glass; however, this option can be expensive. Cover your windows in ballistic film, which is much less expensive than bulletproof glass though still offers a high quality of protection against gunfire. All ballistic film is quick and easy to install and at its best, protects you against breakage from a variety of potential threats, including hammers, bullets, hurricanes, and bombs. If you decide to keep your windows, make sure you have heavy curtains to prevent intruders seeing inside.

The walls of your safe room could hold the highest expense. Bullets from a 9mm firearm can easily penetrate standard internal walls. If you are considering a basement safe room, that's good thinking; corner walls in basements are protected by exterior walls that are often surrounded by concrete and earth. The other two walls will still need reinforcement. In apartments, dividing walls should be fire resistant and are typically made out of cement. There are several ways to reinforce interior walls, including armored steel panels, Kevlar, poured concrete, and sandbags, which can then be covered by a superficial internal wall and is likely to be the most inexpensive option. If these options are too expensive, or just not possible, reinforce your walls with bulky items from inside the safe room. This might include a chest freezer, steel desk, or other large furniture. You can also line your walls with metal filling cabinets or shelves stacked with robust items.

Camouflaging your room isn't essential but it's advised to keep the safe room a secret from dangerous intruders. To truly hide your safe room, you can buy hidden door hinge systems cheaply online that can be used to create a basic bookcase door. If your safe room is in the basement, you can construct a trap door that can be hidden with a rug, and many basements doors can be obscured easily using a clothes stand or other furniture.

Communications:

While the intruders must not know where you are when seeking refuge in your safe room, the safe room must be equipped in a way as to get help to find you. The ability to communicate with the outside world is crucial when retreating to your safe room. These days, most people have cell phones, and this is one of the easiest ways to contact the police or friends. Remember, however, that many cell phones will not have adequate signal underground or in certain areas. Before commencing safe room construction, check the signal of your provider in the safe room while assessing the space. While it's unlikely, intruders can jam cell phone signals. Also, cell phone batteries can be unreliable. Ensure that you have suitable charging capacities in your safe room.

In the event that cell phones become inoperable or otherwise impossible to use, having a landline in your safe room is a good backup option, especially one that doesn't require electricity to operate. Having a computer with Internet access is also a good option since you can call the police using Skype and can easily contact friends and family. A two-way radio is good for short distance contact with a neighbor, while a ham radio is for longer distance communication, though it requires an FCC license.

In addition to keeping in touch with the outside, you'll want to be able to see what's happening on your property while you are safely tucked away. External cameras, motion sensors, automated lights, and monitors in your safe room will give you a good idea of what's going on inside and around the perimeter of your property. If you're investing in cameras, it's a good idea to position one above the main door to your safe room. This way, you can monitor whether or not intruders are attempting to breach your safe room. As with all security measures, make sure that the camera itself is disguised as it could give the location of your safe room away.

Supplies:

You should have adequate food supplies in your safe room to cover a period of 24-48 hours. The safe room is not a bunker. It's only a temporary retreat from danger. While preparing supplies, bear in mind the maximum capacity of the safe room and consider any special dietary and medical requirements. Choose a wide range of food items that do not require cooking or refrigeration. Even if you have an attached bathroom with a water supply, store a minimum of one gallon of water per person. This is just a precautionary measure.

If you're concerned about your food or weapon supply being stolen by intruders or animals, there are effective techniques for keeping your survival cache safe. A survival cache is a hidden stock of goods you'll need in an emergency. Creating said cache is simple; the first and easiest method for hiding your cache is by disguising it as something else. Store canned and packed products in a bin labeled chicken feed, for example. You can also conceal food and supplies behind fake walls, under floorboards, in vents or piping. Make sure you hide your supplies in a place you can easily get to and feel secure inhabiting. Naturally, the best location for your cache is in your safe room.

Ideally, you'll have an attached bathroom and running water for sanitation. If not, you'll need a temporary place to relieve yourself. The best option is a portable camping toilet, which holds around 5 gallons before emptying. Typically, this will do for a 48 hour period. You can also store hand sanitizer, baby wipes, tampons and sanitary pads, diapers and other sanitation equipment.

Safety and health is crucial above all else in extreme situations. Ensure that you have a well-stocked first aid kit just in case you or a member of your group is injured. As well as the first aid kit, store antacids, painkillers, and anti-diarrheal treatments for maximum comfort.

In addition to storing supplies throughout the house, you should also have some emergency supplies in your safe room. This includes a fire extinguisher, goggles, and a particulate mask for each person should a fire break out. You should also store some cold weather gear, including sleeping equipment, just in case your heating cuts out while you're in the safe room.

Entertainment is the final consideration for your safe room supplies, though it is by no means a trivial matter. If you end up spending a couple of days in your safe room, it's important to keep morale high by keeping your mind stimulated with books, games, puzzles, and DVDs. This is especially important if you have children in the safe room.

Finally, if your safety room is breached, your last resort is to defend yourself using force. If an intruder has gone to great lengths to breach your safe room, it's likely that you'll have to defend yourself. Choose your weapons carefully and store additional ammunition in your safe room. Be careful who you assign weapons to in your group. Only those properly trained and licensed should handle firearms. Also, consider stocking close proximity deterrents such as mace and pepper spray in your safe room.

Conclusion

Break-ins are an unpalatable fact of life. Being broken into, in a residential property is obviously more distressing than a burglary in the work place and although vandalism may be rare, the loss of sentimental artefacts can be most upsetting. Prepping your property against intruders requires effective decision making and thorough planning. It is better to take preventative measures as opposed to the 'shutting the stable door after the horse has bolted'. You are far more likely to be burgled if you have been burgled before. Villains are renowned for returning to the same properties.

The most important part of this process is your estimation of what perceivable threats actually exist. If you are merely concerned about your safety, consider non-lethal deterrents including CCTV, monitors, lights, and guard dogs. As explained, crooks, burglars, and/or indeed any intruders, are irresistibly deterred by a burglar alarm more than any other form of home security.

Most of the techniques described in this e-book are only suitable for extreme conditions, such as a natural disaster or widespread social upheaval. This is certainly not an exhaustive list, but hopefully you get the idea. Aside from the techniques described in this book, there are numerous other traps and mechanisms that can be built quickly and easily.

Booby trap is the name of the game in home security. Take a walk around your home. Identify areas where a burglar can hide and vulnerable entry points. Remember, anything you can do to make the crook think twice, make his job more difficult, and rattle his nerves, puts the odds in your favor against a successful home invasion.

www.ingramcontent.com/pod-product-compliance
Lightning Source LLC
Chambersburg PA
CBHW062108280526
45788CB00003B/1397